MR. UNDERVALUED
SILVER

The Brilliance They Refuse to See

ARJ DAUND

I dedicate this book to Mammi, Pappa, Rushi and Kartik,
who kept supporting and loving me throughout the
journey of writing this book!

CONTENTS

1. Hey There, Adventurous soul! 7

2. The Celebration Yet to Come 9

3. Reflections of a Misfit 15

4. Born from Chaos 21

5. Forging Alliances Beyond Earth 27

6. Moments of Magic 33

7. The Soul of SilverSutra 39

8. The Specter of Rejection 46

9. Building Empires with Empathy 53

10. Echoes of Celebration 61

11. Finding Brilliance in Solitude 68

12. Awakening the Inner Warrior 74

You Did It! 83

HEY THERE, ADVENTUROUS SOUL!

Welcome to a wild ride through the unknown realms of imagination and discovery! This book isn't just a collection of words; it's a journey, the kind that spirals into the depths of the strange, the curious, and the utterly bizarre. As I poured my heart and soul into this manuscript, my aim was simple yet profound: to ignite sparks of curiosity and inspire you to uncover the secrets that lie within the pages. You see, this book was conceived during those late-night brainstorming sessions fueled by endless cups of coffee and an insatiable thirst for knowledge. It was a time when the world seemed full of mysteries waiting to be dissected. I dove into countless hours of research, ranging from ancient lore to contemporary issues, all to create a tapestry that you can explore at your own pace. Every chapter is brimming with tales and facts that challenge what you think you know. It's not just about sharing information; it's about inviting you into a dialogue between the past, present, and future. In crafting this book, I reached out to experts, dived into archival treasure troves, and even explored the twists and turns of unconventional thought. Why? Because the treasures they revealed are too tantalizing to keep under wraps. So buckle up! As you explore the twists and turns of this narrative, let your imagination roam free.

The world is a canvas bursting with colors and experiences waiting for you to dip your brush. The journey might just reshape how you see the world — or at least provide a few 'aha!' moments along the way. I want you to feel the thrill of discovery, just as I did while writing this book. It's not just about beauty and facts; it's about understanding the dance between chaos and order, between the seen and the unseen. If you find a nugget of wisdom, a funny anecdote, or a mind-bending paradox, savor it, share it, and let it stew in your thoughts. Remember, reading isn't just a passive experience; it's a conversation, a lovely tango between you and the text. Each page holds the potential to whisk you away into different realms and perspectives that may just stick with you long after you put the book down. And who knows? You might even find that the unknown isn't so frightening after all, but rather a charming companion in your intellectual pursuits. So let's embark on this escapade together, with open minds and curious hearts. This is more than just a book; it's an invitation to explore, a challenge to break down the fences we've built around our understanding. Challenge me, question things, and let's weave the stories of our lives into the fabric of knowledge. Keep that reader's spirit alive! Oh, and don't forget to take breaks, let your imagination collide with reality, and view the world from new angles.

Thank you for choosing to embark on this beautiful chaos with me. I truly can't wait for you to dive into these pages and discover what's waiting for you. Let's turn the curiosity dial to eleven and dive deep into this whirlwind together. You know you want to!

Stay curious,

– ARJ Daund

THE CELEBRATION YET TO COME

A GRAND AFFAIR IN THE MAKING

Raghav Shastri, founder of SilverSutra Technologies, was turning fifty. The halls of his estate gleamed with opulence, chandeliers casting light over golden cutlery and curated centerpieces. A grand celebration was underway, guests from across galaxies gathering to honor his achievements. But amidst the grandeur, Raghav felt a dissonance—his success, though widely celebrated, left a hollow echo inside him.

Wandering into his garden, he questioned the meaning of it all. Was this lavish affair a genuine tribute to his journey—or a mask for unresolved wounds? Memories of a turbulent childhood in Pune, of self-doubt and rejection, clashed with the present moment. The banners showcasing his life felt like curated snapshots, not the raw story he remembered living.

His old friend Arjun arrived, grounding Raghav with a simple truth: "Perhaps both. Success doesn't erase the struggle—it includes it." The evening unfolded with elegance, but Raghav couldn't shake the weight of disconnect. In the laughter and praise, he wondered—would anyone truly see the man beneath the legacy?

As the night deepened, he found meaning not in applause, but in conversations grounded in vulnerability. Surrounded by those who shared his journey—not just the victories but the bruises—he let go of performance and leaned into presence. The celebration slowly transformed into something more intimate: a shared recognition of resilience.

THE WEIGHT OF GREAT EXPECTATIONS

As he stood amidst admirers, Raghav felt the pressure of being not just celebrated—but expected. His internal storm stirred beneath every toast and compliment. The room saw a titan of industry; he saw a man weathered by years of rejection and internalized doubt.

Rain streaked the windows like the tears he rarely allowed. Expectations loomed—those from others, and harsher still, from himself. Even in triumph, he felt unseen. His confidante, Meera, noticed his detachment and gently prompted him to speak.

"It's not just their expectations," he confided. "It's mine. The pressure is suffocating."

"You don't need to perform for anyone," Meera reminded him. "You are not invincible—but you are real. That's enough."

Her words echoed as Raghav turned inward. Perhaps celebration wasn't about accolades, but about reclaiming his own narrative. He began to sense that the weight didn't have to crush him—it could become a compass. True success, he realized, meant embracing the whole journey: scars, solitude, and all.

FACING THE MIRROR

Amid the festivities, Raghav wandered into a quiet corner of the hall, where an ornate mirror stood. Staring at his reflection, he didn't just see a successful entrepreneur. He saw the misfit child, the dreamer from Pune, the man shaped as much by failures as triumphs.

"Who are you, really?" he whispered to the image.

He remembered the late nights spent drafting ideas no one believed in, the rejections, the ridicule. The applause that now surrounded him felt hollow unless he could accept the man behind the success. Standing there, he saw a deeper truth: his worth wasn't tied to achievements—but to resilience, authenticity, and the courage to keep going.

Returning to the crowd, he no longer felt like a performer. He shared stories not just of wins, but of vulnerability. The room shifted from admiration to connection. For the first time in years, he felt free—not because others saw him, but because he finally saw himself.

1. **Business Success Celebration**

   Written Exercises:

   * **Case Study Writing**: Write a case study on a successful startup and how it celebrated a milestone.

   * **Press Release Drafting**: Draft a press release announcing your company's success and celebration plans.

   * **Invitation Design**: Design an invitation card (digital or physical) for the success party.

   * **Budget Planning**: Create a sample budget for a success celebration event with at least 5 cost heads (venue, food, decor, etc.).

   Practical Exercises:

   * **Mock Celebration Planning**: Divide into teams and plan a mock business celebration, assigning roles (planner, finance, PR, hospitality).

   * **Speech Practice**: Deliver a short thank-you speech as a business owner at the celebration.

   * **Success Wall Creation**: Create a "Wall of Achievements" showcasing business milestones visually.

   * **Celebration Proposal**: Prepare and present a proposal with agenda, activities, guest list, and ROI justification.

2. **Guest Hospitality**

   Written Exercises:

   * **Guest Profile Sheet**: Write guest profiles and their preferences (food, seating, welcome style, etc.).

   * **Hospitality Checklist**: Create a checklist for welcoming and taking care of VIP guests.

* **Complaint Handling Report**: Write a report explaining how a hospitality issue (e.g., delay in service) was resolved professionally.

Practical Exercises:

* **Role-play**: Practice welcoming a guest with a proper greeting, offering refreshments, and guiding them.

* **Table Setting**: Arrange a mock hospitality table with name tags, welcome notes, and snacks.

* **Feedback Form Design**: Design a feedback form to collect guest experience after the event.

* **Hospitality Kit Preparation**: Prepare a sample guest kit (thank you note, company brochure, snacks/water, etc.).

3. **Event Management**

Written Exercises:

* **Event Proposal**: Draft a proposal for a corporate event with objective, theme, timeline, and estimated cost.

* **Risk Management Plan**: Write a plan to handle risks (weather, low turnout, technical issues).

* **Vendor List Compilation**: Prepare a list of possible vendors (caterers, decorators, tech support) with contact details.

Practical Exercises:

* **Event Flowchart**: Draw a flowchart/timeline of tasks before, during, and after the event.

* **Team Assignment Drill**: Assign roles in a team (decor, media, logistics, finance) and plan a mini-event.

* **Dry Run**: Conduct a 30-minute mock event with real-time setup, guest welcoming, announcements, and feedback.

* **Event Recap Video/Presentation**: After the event, make a presentation or video summarizing highlights and learning points.

REFLECTIONS OF A MISFIT

IN THE SHADOWS OF GIANTS

Raghav's life, though now lined with success, was forged in the shadows of others. As a student in Pune, he often felt like an outsider—quiet, overlooked, eclipsed by confident classmates like Arjun and Meera. He admired their ease with attention, their natural charisma. He, in contrast, faded into the background.

Despite his silence, creativity bloomed within him. He penned poetry, imagined innovations, and observed life with a depth few noticed. A turning point came during a school talent show. Arjun encouraged him to perform, but Raghav, paralyzed by fear and self-doubt, declined—too afraid to be seen, too afraid to fail.

But not everyone overlooked him. Anjali, a fellow student, invited him to join her study group. Her quiet support planted a seed of belief. In her company, he found his voice. These moments, though small, became lifelines—reminders that even misfits had value.

Years later, as Raghav built his ventures, those early shadows didn't vanish. They became fuel. SilverSutra wasn't just a company—it was a haven for others like him: the overlooked, the underestimated, the misfits who dared to dream anyway.

MOMENTS OF CLARITY

Years later, in a small, cluttered room filled with sketches and startup plans, Raghav reflected on the identity he had carved. As a child, he had been dismissed. As a teen, laughed at for saying he wanted to invent things that changed lives. But those moments, painful as they were, gave him a kind of clarity.

He recalled a rainy afternoon in a Pune café when he shared his dreams with friends who mocked him. Their dismissal stung—but it awakened a quiet resolve. He realized that his path wasn't meant to be understood by everyone. It wasn't meant to follow convention.

A key mentor, Mr. Iyer, once told him: "Swim upstream, Raghav. The best inventions come from those who dare to see what others don't." Those words stuck. They fueled his desire to build empathetic, human-centered technologies. His company WiredMind was born from that very principle: to create with compassion.

Another catalyst came from Chitra, a pioneer in mental health tech. She told him: "Your struggles are your strength. They help you build what the world needs but doesn't know how to ask for." Inspired, Raghav launched the Collective Misfit Network— offering community and mentorship for those like him, who never fit in, yet carried extraordinary potential.

His journey was no longer about proving his worth. It became about helping others find theirs.

THE ROAD LESS TRAVELED

Raghav stood at the edge of a choice—conform, or risk everything for the road less traveled. He chose risk.

His entrepreneurial story began modestly—handmade wallets crafted from recycled materials. People laughed. Friends questioned his decisions. Sales were slow. But he persisted, powered by purpose and a refusal to fit into traditional molds.

An important collaboration came through Meera, a young artist who inspired him to combine creativity with sustainability. Together, they hosted workshops blending art and activism. That effort sparked a new idea—entrepreneurship driven by empathy, not just profit.

This became the foundation for his business philosophy. Raghav poured himself into understanding markets, emotions, and the pulse of human needs. He learned that true innovation required emotional intelligence as much as strategy. Through long nights and lonely sacrifices, he built not just a company— but a movement.

In choosing the road less traveled, Raghav didn't just change his life. He created space for others to walk their own paths, too.

1. **Reflection on Weaknesses**

   Written Exercises:

   * **Self-Audit Journal**: Write a one-page reflection identifying 3 personal/professional weaknesses and how they affect your performance.

   * **SWOT Analysis**: Complete a personal SWOT analysis with detailed weaknesses and how to work on them.

   * **Failure Reflection Letter**: Write a letter to your future self describing a past failure, what you learned, and how you plan to improve.

   Practical Exercises:

   * **Peer Feedback Session**: Sit in pairs and give constructive feedback on each other's weak areas.

   * **Weakness to Strength Activity**: Choose a weakness and create a step-by-step improvement plan with deadlines.

   * **Mirror Talk Drill**: Practice speaking 3 identified weaknesses and 3 ways you'll overcome them — aloud, in front of a mirror.

   * **Role-Reversal Game**: Act out a weakness scenario, then replay it by applying improvement strategies.

2. **Optimistic Perception**

   Written Exercises:

   * **Positive Reframing Practice**: Take 3 negative statements and rewrite them in an optimistic tone.

   * **Gratitude List**: List 10 things you're grateful for today and explain how each brings a positive impact.

* **Optimism Diary**: Maintain a 7-day journal capturing only the positive outcomes and learnings from each day.

Practical Exercises:

* **Compliment Circle**: Sit in a circle and give one positive quality or compliment to each participant.

* **"Yes, and..." Game**: A communication game where every response must start with "Yes, and..." to build optimistic conversations.

* **Vision Board Making**: Create a vision board of your dreams, goals, and future with positive affirmations and images.

* **Optimism Role Play**: Act out a tough situation (like job rejection) and how you would stay hopeful through it.

3. **Past vs Now vs Future**

Written Exercises:

* **Timeline Reflection**: Create a 3-column table: *Past Habits, Current Changes, Future Aspirations.*

* **Letter Series**: Write three letters — to your past self, present self, and future self.

* **Learning Milestone Map**: Draw a map showing 5 key lessons learned in the past, how they helped now, and how they'll guide your future.

Practical Exercises:

* **Growth Graph**: Plot your personal or professional growth on a line graph (marking age/stage on the X-axis).

* **Then vs Now Talk**: Share a 2-minute speech comparing your mindset/skills before and now.

* **"Time Travel" Interviews**: One student plays the past-you, one the present-you, and one the future-you in a group interview.

* **Goal Ladder**: Draw a ladder with past efforts as steps, current skills as support, and future goals at the top.

BORN FROM CHAOS

Raghav's story didn't begin with triumph—it began in the ruins of uncertainty. His life was not shaped by a silver spoon, but by the rusted tools of hardship and survival. Raised in the crowded and narrow streets of Pune, his childhood was marked by the kind of turbulence that often erases dreams before they are even imagined. Crumbling walls, flickering lights, and the everpresent buzz of scooters and voices filled his early world. The household he grew up in was modest, sometimes even barely functional. Finances were fragile, as if held together by invisible strings that could snap at any moment. His parents, though well-meaning, were often consumed by their own struggles—his father juggling multiple jobs and his mother overwhelmed by the weight of trying to keep the family whole. In such an environment, emotional warmth was a scarce resource.

Loneliness, however, was never silent. It echoed loudly in Raghav's mind, especially in moments when his questions went unanswered or when his quiet victories—like learning a difficult word or fixing a broken toy—went unnoticed. The early years were marked by a gnawing sense of being unheard and unseen, as if he existed in the margins of his own story. For a child, invisibility is a kind of slow erasure, and Raghav felt it deeply. Yet, rather than turn bitter, he began to observe. If he wasn't being listened to, he decided he would listen—to everything. The people around him, their stories, their silences, their pain, their laughter—he soaked it all in like a sponge.

Amid the chaos, there were slivers of light—thin, almost imperceptible threads of hope that stitched themselves into the fabric of his soul. A schoolteacher who noticed how well he wrote and encouraged him to keep going, even when his grades faltered. A local librarian who let him linger in the reading corner long after his borrowing time was up. The pages of those books became his sanctuary, their characters his companions. They whispered to him about possibility, about worlds far beyond the confines of his narrow lane. There were even strangers—an old woman who offered him food when she saw him walking home alone in the rain, a street vendor who let him read comics at his stall without paying. These acts, small and scattered, left deep impressions.

He began to understand something profound: chaos didn't have to destroy—it could teach. In fact, it had already begun to shape his inner scaffolding. The very circumstances that could have broken him were the ones forging his resilience. The unpredictability of his life trained him to adapt, to stay alert, and to create opportunity where there seemed to be none. He learned to problem-solve on the fly, to negotiate with limited resources, to think creatively not because it was encouraged, but because it was necessary.

By the time he was a teenager, Raghav had already developed a quiet sort of strength. He didn't speak much in large groups, but when he did, people listened. There was something about him—an intensity tempered with empathy, a confidence born not of privilege, but of perseverance. He began to mentor younger students in his neighborhood, helping them with schoolwork and telling them stories that combined myth, memory, and imagination. He saw himself in them—the confusion, the fear, and the desperate desire to rise.

Rather than run from his past, Raghav chose to embrace it. He understood that pretending to come from a polished background would be a betrayal not only of the truth, but of the gifts his circumstances had given him. The streets had taught him survival, yes — but also ingenuity, empathy, and grit. He began to see chaos not as a curse, but as a raw material. Something that could be shaped, harnessed, and turned into meaning.

Years later, when Raghav would go on to build a community center for underserved youth in the very neighborhood he came from, people would ask him where his journey began. And he would smile — not with pride, but with recognition — and say, "In the cracks." He knew that beauty often grows in the most unlikely places. The boy born from chaos had not only survived it; he had transformed it. And in doing so, he became a symbol of what is possible when we refuse to let our beginnings define our endings.

1. **Struggles Faced Since Childhood**

Written Exercises:

* **Life Journey Story**: Write a short story titled *"My Journey So Far: From Struggles to Strengths"*.

* **Childhood Struggle Reflection**: List 3 major struggles you faced in childhood and what each taught you.

* **Trigger Tracker**: Journal past childhood events that still affect your emotions or decisions today.

Practical Exercises:

* **Story Sharing Circle**: In small groups, share one childhood struggle and how you overcame or are coping with it.

* **Timeline Activity**: Draw a personal timeline marking 5 key struggles and how you grew through each.

* **Symbol Drawing**: Create a symbolic drawing or sketch representing your childhood struggle and current self.

* **Healing Affirmation Circle**: Speak one positive affirmation to your "younger self" in front of a mirror or group.

2. **Conflict Management with Those with Low or Unclear Vision**

("Low vision" here means unclear goals or limited mindset, not visual impairment.)

Written Exercises:

* **Conflict Case Study**: Write about a real conflict with someone having a fixed/negative mindset. What went wrong? What could be done better?

* **Communication Strategy Plan**: Outline a strategy for resolving conflict through empathy and clarity when dealing with narrow-minded or confused individuals.

* **Empathy Chart**: Create a chart listing 3 people with unclear vision, their concerns, and how you can approach them empathetically.

Practical Exercises:

* **Role Play: Mindset Clash**: One person acts as a visionary, another as a limited thinker. Practice resolving the disagreement.

* **Active Listening Drill**: Practice active listening with someone sharing a limited view, and try responding without judgment.

* **Reframing Game**: Take 3 common negative statements and reframe them into solution-focused statements.

* **Debate Simulation**: Conduct a mock meeting where conflicting views are resolved through guided discussion.

3. **Keeping a Company of Elite or Success Mindset**

Written Exercises:

* **Ideal Circle Mapping**: Draw your "circle of influence." Highlight who inspires growth and who needs boundaries.

* **Elite Influence Essay**: Write an essay titled *"The People I Want to Learn From"* describing the qualities of successful mentors or peers.

* **Networking Plan**: Draft a weekly/monthly plan to connect with high-mindset people (events, reading, mentorship, etc.).

Practical Exercises:

✳ **Success Circle Meetup**: Host a mock mastermind session where each participant shares one goal and one challenge.

✳ **Positive Influence Role Play**: Act out a conversation between a goal-setter and an achiever. Observe language, tone, and mindset.

✳ **Digital Clean-up Challenge**: Ask learners to review and filter their social media/following list to align with a success mindset.

✳ **Shadow a Mentor Activity**: Organize a short activity where students/internees follow or research a successful person and share 3 learnings.

FORGING ALLIANCES BEYOND EARTH

As Raghav's ventures expanded, so too did the dimensions of his ambition. What had once begun as a deeply personal mission — a lone pursuit to escape the gravity of his past and prove his worth — evolved into something far greater. The hunger for achievement gave way to a longing for impact. The further he journeyed, the more he understood that no true success existed in isolation. Real change required connection — bold, sometimes uncomfortable, always expansive.

His work began attracting attention — not only from business circles in India, but from innovators around the world. Invitations followed: conferences in Amsterdam, think tanks in Nairobi, roundtables in Tokyo. But Raghav didn't just attend. He listened. He questioned. He sought out the minds that didn't think like his. These weren't mere professional contacts. They were cultural disruptors, visionaries, and in some cases, challengers of his worldview. The diversity of thought, shaped by geography, history, and discipline, became a catalyst for his evolution.

Then, came the shift that would define his second act: he stopped networking for recognition and started forging alliances for transformation. These relationships weren't about leveraging influence, but about exchanging wisdom. Conversations with space scientists about off-planet sustainability inspired his local environmental initiatives. Dialogues with indigenous leaders reshaped how he approached community development. He partnered with tech leaders to design tools for education in areas still struggling with basic connectivity.

The metaphor that had once seemed like science fiction—of "reaching beyond Earth"—became the perfect frame for his journey. Not because he was literally launching rockets, but because he was building bridges across seemingly unbridgeable divides. To him, a scientist from Finland, a farmer in Odisha, and a coder from Kenya all inhabited different worlds—planets of thought, culture, and belief. Yet through curiosity, humility, and dialogue, they became part of his orbit.

These cosmic alliances weren't built overnight. They required vulnerability—the courage to admit what he didn't know. But it was in these spaces of uncertainty that growth happened. No longer obsessed with always being the smartest in the room, Raghav now strived to be the most teachable. This mindset shift brought him face to face with three truths that became the compass for all his interactions:

1. **Network with purpose, not pretense.**

   Raghav realized that the most valuable relationships came not from the clinking of glasses at corporate galas, but from honest, sometimes quiet conversations over shared dreams. He stopped measuring people by titles and started seeking resonance—people who aligned with values, not just metrics. He learned to ask: *What can we build together?* instead of *What can I gain from you?*

2. **Never see yourself as smaller than anyone.**

   In the early days, self-doubt often whispered that he didn't belong in rooms with Nobel laureates or CEOs. But the more he engaged, the more he saw the humanity behind the accolades. Everyone, no matter how brilliant, had blind spots. And sometimes, it was his story—from the streets of Pune, from chaos to clarity—that offered a perspective they hadn't considered. He brought something no one else could: lived insight born from struggle and reinvention.

3. **Great ideas are born from unlikely discussions.**

Raghav learned to lean into discomfort—the conversations that didn't immediately make sense, the collaborations that seemed improbable. Whether it was exploring AI ethics with a Buddhist monk or brainstorming clean energy solutions with teenage coders, he discovered that innovation thrives at intersections. It's in the space between differences that truly original ideas take root.

In time, these global conversations coalesced into something more powerful than a network—they became his constellation. A web of relationships, glimmering like stars in an ever-expanding sky, each one illuminating a different facet of his mission. Some offered mentorship. Others offered challenge. All offered possibility.

With this constellation behind him, Raghav began to dream bigger than companies or profits. He thought in terms of ecosystems, legacies, and generations. His ventures became vessels for shared purpose. His leadership evolved into stewardship—not of an empire, but of a movement. He understood that real power wasn't about how high you could go, but how far you could reach, and who you could bring with you.

In a world increasingly divided by borders and beliefs, Raghav had chosen the opposite path: radical connection. He wasn't just forging alliances across industries or countries. He was stitching together fragments of humanity, crafting something that felt—at its best—like unity.

The boy who had once walked alone in the alleys of Pune had now become a bridge between worlds.

1. **Networking Strategies**

   Written Exercises:

   * **Personal Elevator Pitch**: Write a 30-second pitch about who you are, what you do, and what value you bring.

   * **Networking Plan**: List 3 events, 5 platforms (like LinkedIn), and 5 people you want to connect with over the next month.

   * **Email/DM Drafting**: Practice writing a professional introduction message to a mentor or expert in your field.

   Practical Exercises:

   * **Networking Role Play**: Simulate meeting someone at an event. Practice initiating a conversation and exchanging contacts.

   * **Business Card Activity**: Design your own business card with key details and branding.

   * **"Find a Match" Drill**: Each person is given a profession or skill—they must network with others to find 2–3 beneficial connections.

   * **Follow-up Simulation**: Practice sending a follow-up message/email after a networking event.

2. **Never Feeling Self as Less Powerful**

   Written Exercises:

   * **Affirmation Writing**: Write 5 affirmations about your worth, skills, and potential.

   * **Strength Resume**: Create a resume of your strengths, experiences, talents, and wins—even informal ones.

* **Rejection Reframing Journal**: Describe a situation where you felt rejected and write what you *learned* instead.

Practical Exercises:

* **Mirror Confidence Drill**: Speak aloud 3 strengths and 1 goal in front of a mirror with power posture.

* **Power Walk Challenge**: Walk confidently across the room while holding eye contact and smiling—small but impactful.

* **Compliment Exchange**: Pair up and give each other genuine, strength-based compliments.

* **"I Am Proud Because…" Round**: Each person completes this sentence out loud to the group.

3. **Discussing Ideas with Great People**

Written Exercises:

* **Email to a Thought Leader**: Draft an email proposing a meaningful question or topic to discuss with a mentor.

* **Top 5 Questions List**: Prepare a list of intelligent, curious questions you would ask a successful person in your field.

* **Meeting Agenda Draft**: Imagine you are invited to a roundtable with successful people—draft an agenda with your talking points.

Practical Exercises:

* **Mock Mastermind Session**: Form a group of "great thinkers" (students or team) and each shares one idea/ problem for feedback.

* **Idea Pitch Exercise**: Present an innovative idea in under 3 minutes to a group and invite critique.

* **Role-play as a Visionary**: One student plays a successful entrepreneur, the other asks bold, idea-based questions.

* **Panel Simulation**: Set up a mock panel discussion with 3 "great people" (students act as experts) and 1 moderator.

MOMENTS OF MAGIC

Amidst the whirlwind of innovation, collaboration, and relentless progress, Raghav began to notice something strange—quiet moments that seemed to shimmer outside of time. They weren't planned, measured, or optimized. They arrived softly, often unannounced, and yet they left a deeper impact than the most celebrated milestones. These moments didn't follow logic. Some would call them coincidence. Others, fate. Raghav began to call them magic.

One such moment came during an unremarkable layover in Bhutan. He'd been invited to speak at a summit on sustainable development, but his flight was delayed, rerouted, and finally grounded overnight. Frustrated and restless, he wandered the quiet outskirts of the monastery where he was staying. That's when he met the monk.

The man seemed ancient, but his eyes danced like stars. They spoke for less than ten minutes, mostly in silence. As Raghav prepared to leave, the monk placed a hand gently on his shoulder and said, "To build the future, you must first heal the past."

It was a sentence, no more than a dozen words. But it struck Raghav like thunder. It echoed within him long after he left Bhutan—through airports, meetings, and late-night strategy sessions. That simple truth unraveled something in him. He had spent so many years running toward the future, fueled by the hunger to *become*, that he had never paused to examine what he was running *from*.

The monk's words ignited a different kind of journey—not outward, but inward. He didn't announce it, or post about it, or make it part of any keynote speech. It was deeply personal. Quiet. He began to explore healing, not as a retreat from ambition, but as its deeper foundation. Meditation, something he had once dismissed as a luxury for the idle, became his daily discipline. Breathwork, silence, ancient texts, and energy practices slowly replaced his morning news scrolls and performance metrics.

For the first time in years, he allowed himself to *be* rather than constantly *do*. He stopped chasing clarity in spreadsheets and began to find it in stillness. He sat with old wounds—the sense of abandonment from childhood, the pressure to prove his worth, the guilt of early mistakes made in haste. And instead of pushing them away, he began to hold space for them. He didn't fix them, exactly. He acknowledged them. And in that acknowledgment, they began to soften.

As he healed, his energy changed. He didn't need to force results anymore. Meetings felt more fluid, less combative. His teams noticed first—how he listened differently, how he responded with presence rather than urgency. Projects that had once been driven by deadlines now unfolded with greater ease, as if aligned with a larger rhythm. Investors remarked on his clarity. Collaborators marveled at his intuition. And for the first time in years, Raghav's body responded with health instead of fatigue. Sleep deepened. Stress released. There was less noise in his mind, and more space in his heart.

He came to a humbling realization: transformation doesn't start in boardrooms or on balance sheets. It begins within. Real innovation—sustainable, soulful innovation—emerges not from burnout or competition, but from inner alignment. As he evolved inwardly, the world around him began to shift as well. New opportunities arose without hustle. People arrived in his life without agenda. Joy, once occasional and fleeting, became steady and quiet.

He no longer saw himself merely as an entrepreneur or a leader. He began to sense he was a vessel—part of something larger, moving through him rather than from him. His mission, once framed by metrics and milestones, now included grace, empathy, and presence. He spoke less of disruption, more of harmony. He didn't abandon ambition—he refined it.

In interviews, when asked about the most valuable thing he ever created, Raghav would smile gently. People expected him to talk about his company, his patents, or his social initiatives. But his answer surprised them.

"The most magical thing I ever created," he'd say, "was my own rebirth."

Not a reinvention. Not a brand refresh. A rebirth. A return to self. To stillness. To purpose without noise.

Because sometimes, the most radical transformation doesn't come from reaching farther out—but from journeying deeper in.

1. **Spiritual Experience**

   Written Exercises:

   ✳ **Spiritual Moment Journal**: Write about a moment when you felt deeply connected to something greater than yourself.

   ✳ **Sacred Space Reflection**: Describe a place (real or imagined) where you feel spiritually safe and peaceful.

   ✳ **Gratitude Letter to the Universe**: Pen a letter expressing thanks to life, God, or nature for your journey so far.

   Practical Exercises:

   ✳ **5-Minute Silent Meditation**: Practice silent sitting with focus on breathing or a calming word (like "peace").

   ✳ **Nature Connection Walk**: Take a walk observing sounds, sights, and sensations mindfully—record your thoughts afterward.

   ✳ **Guided Visualization**: Use a script to guide students through a spiritual visualization journey (e.g., meeting a wise inner guide).

   ✳ **Chanting/Prayer Circle**: Recite or listen to simple chants or affirmations that create a sense of unity and calm.

2. **Healing Inside**

   Written Exercises:

   ✳ **Pain-to-Power Story**: Write about an emotional wound and how it made you stronger.

   ✳ **Heart Letter**: Write a letter to someone (you may or may not send it) to forgive or release emotional pain.

✳ **Inner Child Dialogue**: Write a conversation between your adult self and your inner child, offering comfort and healing.

Practical Exercises:

✳ **Self-Hug Activity**: Place hands on your heart and gently say a healing affirmation like "I am safe. I am healing."

✳ **Tear-and-Throw**: Write your emotional pain on paper, tear it, and throw it in a symbolic release ritual.

✳ **Soothing Sounds Session**: Play calming music or healing frequencies and ask participants to journal feelings afterward.

✳ **Healing Circle**: Sit in a circle; each person shares one thing they are healing from (optional) and gets a moment of silent support.

3. **Energising Cells**

Written Exercises:

✳ **Energy Inventory**: List activities/people/foods that energize you vs. those that drain you.

✳ **Power Statement**: Write a sentence beginning with "When I feel energized, I can…" and complete it with purpose.

✳ **Cell Rejuvenation Visualization Script**: Write or read a short visualization imagining each cell in your body lighting up with energy.

Practical Exercises:

✳ **Power Movement Drill**: Do 2–3 minutes of energizing movement (e.g., stretches, jumping jacks, power poses).

✳ **Breath of Fire (Kapalabhati)**: Practice short, fast, rhythmic breaths to stimulate energy and focus (under guidance).

✳ **Sun Bathing/Morning Routine**: Step outside in sunlight for 5 minutes with slow breaths and intention-setting.

✳ **Laughter Therapy**: Do 3 minutes of forced-to-natural laughter — relieves stress and energizes body cells.

THE SOUL OF SILVERSUTRA

SilverSutra Technologies wasn't born from spreadsheets or market analysis. It wasn't conceived in a boardroom or crafted from a strategic business plan. No, SilverSutra was born from heartbreak—a raw, vulnerable place that many would shy away from, but which Raghav embraced as his source of transformation.

The catalyst for his journey came from the personal devastation of a failed relationship—a loss that shattered the very foundation of his emotional world. It wasn't just the end of love. It was the collapse of his vision of the future. The person he thought he would share his life with, the dreams they had built together, and the future he had envisioned—all of it crumbled into an abyss of grief. For months, Raghav wrestled with an emptiness that seemed to stretch endlessly before him. He felt broken, small, and unsure of how to move forward. Yet, in the depths of his sorrow, something unexpected began to stir.

Rather than allowing grief to consume him, Raghav chose to transform it. Instead of retreating into isolation, he leaned into the pain. He found solace in the quiet moments, in the hum of the city's streets, in the quiet hours spent thinking about what had truly mattered in his life. In that solitude, he began to piece together something greater than the loss itself. He realized that his pain could be a catalyst for purpose, that his journey from darkness could illuminate the path for others.

This newfound clarity led him to a simple, yet profound vision: he would create a company not just for the sake of profit, but for something more. SilverSutra would be built with a heart and soul that reflected the very essence of what he had come to understand in his own healing journey. It would be a company rooted in empathy, resilience, and the deep belief that every person, no matter their past or present, deserved to feel valued. Raghav's vision wasn't just to serve markets or clients, but to serve people—especially those who felt invisible, undervalued, or forgotten. He knew what it felt like to be overlooked, and he wanted SilverSutra to be a place where people could find purpose, dignity, and empowerment.

With this vision in mind, Raghav established three founding principles that would become the bedrock of SilverSutra's identity:

1. **Solve real, long-term problems.**

   SilverSutra wouldn't be driven by trends or the chase for the next big thing. Raghav knew that the world didn't need more products—it needed solutions that could stand the test of time. The focus would always be on solving the problems that mattered most, the ones that affected people deeply. Whether it was a groundbreaking technology, an innovative service, or a new approach to old problems, SilverSutra would exist to create tangible, meaningful impact that lasted far beyond the surface level.

2. **Offer people more than products—offer them purpose.**

   Raghav understood that people didn't just want to consume; they wanted to connect to something larger than themselves. SilverSutra's products would never be mere commodities. They would carry the essence of the company's deeper purpose. Each product would be a tool to empower individuals, help them discover their own potential, and make their lives better. Whether it was through technology that improved lives or a culture that inspired creativity and resilience, the company's purpose would always be intertwined with the lives of the people it touched.

3.   **Let every setback refine, not define.**

SilverSutra was destined for challenges. Raghav knew this. But instead of seeing setbacks as roadblocks, he chose to view them as opportunities for growth. Every failure, every misstep, would be an opportunity to refine the company's vision and approach. The journey would be long, the road would be rocky, but each moment of adversity would make SilverSutra stronger, more resilient, and more aligned with its mission. He refused to let failure define the company or its people. Instead, he allowed it to shape them into something even better.

With these principles guiding him, Raghav poured his heart into the creation of SilverSutra. The company quickly became more than just a business. It became a reflection of his soul, his experiences, and his relentless belief in human resilience. It embodied a deep commitment to never giving up, even when life's circumstances seemed insurmountable. SilverSutra wasn't just about technological innovation—it was about personal transformation, both for Raghav and for everyone who became part of the company's journey.

Through every challenge, every late-night brainstorming session, and every pivot the company made, SilverSutra remained grounded in its core beliefs. It became a place where empathy, purpose, and resilience weren't just buzzwords—they were the foundation of everything they did. The company began to attract people who shared that same belief—that success was not only about profits, but about making the world a better place for everyone.

Years later, as SilverSutra grew into a successful and impactful enterprise, Raghav would look back at its humble beginnings and marvel at how far they had come. It wasn't just a company anymore. It was a testament to the power of transformation—the story of a soul that refused to break, and instead, chose to rise, rebuild, and create something beautiful from the ashes of heartbreak.

SilverSutra wasn't just a business. It was the embodiment of a soul's strength and resilience—a company built not from the desire for success, but from the need to heal, to give, and to serve something greater than oneself.

1. **Founder of Startup**

   Written Exercises:

   * **Startup Vision Sheet**: Write your mission, vision, and what inspired you to start this venture.

   * **Problem-Solution Statement**: Clearly define the problem you're solving and how your startup addresses it.

   * **Founder's Story**: Write a first-person narrative titled *"Why I Started This"* describing your journey.

   Practical Exercises:

   * **Pitch Practice**: Deliver a 60-second startup pitch to peers or mentors.

   * **Logo & Name Design**: Create a name and rough logo sketch representing your brand's core purpose.

   * **Roleplay: Investor Meet**: Simulate a meeting where you're the founder and others are potential investors asking questions.

   * **Startup Calendar**: Make a 30-day launch plan with 1 action step per day.

2. **USP (Unique Selling Proposition)**

   Written Exercises:

   * **USP in One Line**: Write a one-line sentence describing what makes your product or service different and better.

   * **Competitor Analysis**: Compare your idea to 2 similar existing ones and identify your edge.

   * **Customer Value List**: List 5 core values or benefits customers get from your offering.

Practical Exercises:

* **USP Testing Booth**: Present your USP to 3–5 people and collect feedback—do they understand and find it compelling?

* **Elevator Pitch Drill**: Explain your USP in 30 seconds to different "audiences" (a child, a busy executive, a friend).

* **Tagline Creation Workshop**: Write 3 creative taglines capturing your USP.

3. **Ideas That Solve Long-Term Problems**

Written Exercises:

* **Problem-Solver Journal**: Pick a long-term social or economic issue and write how your startup could contribute to solving it.

* **Impact Map**: Draw a cause-effect diagram showing how your idea leads to long-term improvement.

* **Vision 2035 Statement**: Describe how your idea will still be relevant and helpful 10 years from now.

Practical Exercises:

* **Future Backward Exercise**: Start from the year 2035 and map backwards how your idea evolved to bring lasting change.

* **UN SDG Matchmaking**: Match your startup idea to one or more of the UN Sustainable Development Goals.

* **Feedback from Elders**: Present your long-term idea to someone from an older generation and get perspective on sustainability.

* **Prototype Think Tank**: Build a mock model of your solution using paper, PPT, or digital tool to show how it works over time.

THE SPECTER OF REJECTION

Even after his greatest achievements, even with SilverSutra flourishing and recognition pouring in, the specter of rejection still haunted Raghav. The memories of the early days—of every investor who turned him down, every partner who walked away, and every cold, dismissive glance from the people who couldn't see his potential—remained etched deeply in his psyche. Those moments, once painful and raw, continued to echo through his mind like the distant rumble of a thunderstorm. They had been the soundtrack of his early career, and their ghostly presence never quite left.

At first, Raghav had believed that success would somehow erase the sting of those rejections. That once he achieved his dreams, the past would fade into obscurity. But the truth was far more complicated. The scars of rejection were not so easily erased. They were ingrained, not in the fabric of his work, but in the contours of his self-worth. Every time he sat at a table with high-profile investors or partners, there was a subtle, persistent voice whispering, "You weren't good enough then. What makes you think you're good enough now?"

But Raghav had a choice: he could allow rejection to dictate his sense of worth, or he could transform it. He refused to be shackled by the "no's" of the past. Instead, he chose to use them as tools—tools for growth, self-reflection, and evolution.

He began to write. Not for his blog, not for his business, but for himself. Every failure, every painful rejection, was documented in his journal. He wrote about the emails that were never answered, the meetings that ended in polite but firm "nos," the partnerships that never materialized. But he didn't stop at just recounting the events. He studied them, dissected them, and began to see patterns — not in the rejection itself, but in his response to it. What was it about his approach, his mindset, or his communication that had triggered those rejections? What could he learn from those experiences to avoid the same pitfalls moving forward?

Through this process, Raghav discovered something profound: rejection wasn't weakness. It wasn't a personal failing. Instead, it was feedback — a message from the universe telling him what wasn't aligned with his journey yet, or what he still needed to learn. It wasn't a verdict on his worth as a person; it was a signal that he hadn't found the right fit, the right opportunity, or the right timing. Rejection became a lens through which he could gain clarity.

He began to ask himself different questions after each rejection:

* **Is this rejection about me — or their vision?**

   * He realized that often, a "no" wasn't about his abilities, but about the vision, needs, or timing of the other person. Perhaps they were seeking something he couldn't offer at that moment. Or perhaps, they just weren't able to see his potential. But it didn't mean he wasn't enough. It simply meant the fit wasn't there yet.

* **What truth is hiding in this "no"?**

   * Rejection, he learned, was an opportunity to confront uncomfortable truths. Did his pitch lack clarity? Was his vision too ambitious for the time being? Were there aspects of his approach that needed refinement? Rather

than wallowing in self-doubt, he began to approach rejection with curiosity. What could he learn from the rejection that would make him better next time?

✳ **What's my next step, anyway?**

♦ Rejection, he came to understand, wasn't an ending — it was merely a stepping stone. So many times, rejection had led him down unexpected paths that ultimately brought him to better opportunities. Each "no" simply meant that a different "yes" was waiting somewhere ahead. And with each rejection, he got one step closer to the right fit, the right partnership, the right breakthrough.

With this mindset shift, Raghav no longer saw rejection as a reflection of his failure, but as an essential part of the journey — a necessary feedback loop that honed him into a stronger, more focused version of himself. He didn't seek to avoid rejection; he embraced it. He knew that every rejection was a tool, and every "no" was an opportunity to learn, adapt, and grow stronger.

And, over time, something remarkable happened. The very people who once dismissed him, who had doubted him and turned him away, began to notice his growth. They came knocking — sometimes in surprise, sometimes with a sense of awe. They saw the company he had built, the vision he had articulated, and the resilience he had displayed. They saw the man he had become. But by then, Raghav had grown beyond his need for validation. His self-worth was no longer tied to the approval of others. His worth came from within, from the quiet confidence that was forged in the fires of rejection.

The investors who had once rejected him now wanted to be part of his success. The partners who had walked away now sought him out for collaboration. And Raghav, having been forged in the fires of doubt and rejection, stood tall — not in spite of those rejections, but because of them. He had learned to rise, not because of success, but because of how he had faced the very things that sought to bring him down.

Raghav understood, at last, that rejection wasn't the end. It was, in fact, the beginning of something greater. It was the moment when the universe asked, "Are you ready for what's next?" And with each rejection, he had answered, "Yes."

1. Facing Rejections

Written Exercises:

* **Rejection Reflection Journal**: Write about a time when you faced rejection. What were your initial thoughts, and how did you cope?

* **Rejection Reframe**: For every rejection you've faced, list 2 lessons you learned from it.

* **Letter of Gratitude to Rejection**: Write a letter thanking the rejection for teaching you something important.

Practical Exercises:

* **Role-Play Rejection Response**: Simulate a scenario where you get rejected (e.g., a job offer, project proposal). Practice responding with grace and understanding.

* **Rejection Affirmation**: Stand in front of a mirror and say, "Rejection is just redirection. I am growing."

* **Rejection Journal**: For a week, write down every instance of rejection or failure and how you responded positively.

* **Support Group Discussion**: In a group, share a personal rejection story and discuss how each person dealt with it.

2. Emerging Back

Written Exercises:

* **Bounce Back Story**: Write about a time when you experienced failure but managed to rise again. What steps did you take to recover?

* **Strengths in Adversity**: List 5 personal strengths that helped you bounce back from tough situations.

* **Future Vision Statement**: Write about how you envision yourself after facing a setback. What will you achieve next?

Practical Exercises:

* **Visualizing Comeback**: Sit quietly for 5 minutes and visualize a time when you overcame failure. Reflect on the steps you took and the feeling of success that followed.

* **Resilience Action Plan**: Write down 3 concrete steps you will take next time you face failure or a setback.

* **Power Pose Exercise**: Stand in a power pose for 2 minutes after a setback. It boosts confidence and mental toughness.

* **Positive Affirmation Cards**: Create a set of 5 affirmations or motivational quotes that you can refer to when bouncing back from difficulties.

3. **Never Letting Off**

Written Exercises:

* **Persistence Story**: Write about a time when you didn't give up, even when things got tough. What motivated you to keep going?

* **Unyielding Goal Worksheet**: List a goal you've been working toward for a long time. What's your plan for sticking with it, no matter the obstacles?

* **Perseverance Motivation List**: Write down 5 reasons why you should never let go of your goals, even when it seems hard.

* *Practical Exercises:*

* **Accountability Partner Exercise**: Pair up with someone and share a long-term goal. Set regular check-ins to keep each other motivated and committed.

✳ **Time Blocking for Persistence**: Break down your long-term goal into daily, small tasks. Dedicate a fixed amount of time each day to work toward it, no matter how small.

✳ **Daily Gratitude Practice**: Each day, write down 3 things you are grateful for. This will build your mental resilience and keep you moving forward.

✳ **Personal Motivation Playlist**: Create a playlist of songs or podcasts that inspire you. Listen to it when you feel like giving up.

BUILDING EMPIRES WITH EMPATHY

As SilverSutra scaled, Raghav found himself confronted with a new and unexpected challenge: how to lead without becoming the kind of boss he once feared.

In the early days of his career, Raghav had worked under leaders who seemed to thrive on control and fear. They were figures of authority who ruled with a heavy hand, fostering an atmosphere of competition rather than collaboration. Employees were viewed as cogs in a machine, expendable and replaceable, rather than as people with individual needs, aspirations, and vulnerabilities. For Raghav, this type of leadership was both stifling and demoralizing. It created an environment where innovation was discouraged, and human connection was relegated to the background in favor of deadlines, profits, and metrics.

As SilverSutra began to grow, Raghav knew that he did not want to repeat this cycle. He had seen firsthand the damage done when leadership was driven by fear. He knew that to build something sustainable, something meaningful, he needed to take a different approach—one that put people first. His vision wasn't just about creating the next big tech company; it was about fostering an environment where individuals could thrive, both personally and professionally.

But the question was: how?

In the tech world, where so many companies were driven by performance metrics and bottom-line results, the concept of empathy in leadership felt like an anomaly. It was a risky proposition, one that could easily be misunderstood as weakness or inefficiency. Many around him cautioned against it. They advised him to adopt a more traditional, top-down approach—demanding respect from his teams through authority and control. They argued that leaders needed to project strength, not vulnerability, and that power was something to be wielded, not shared.

But Raghav had already experienced the consequences of leadership rooted in fear, and he refused to perpetuate that cycle. He understood something that many in the business world didn't: true leadership wasn't about dominance—it was about connection. It was about building relationships and creating an environment where people could thrive. So, rather than following the traditional models of authority, he chose to lead with empathy.

Empathy became the cornerstone of Raghav's leadership philosophy. He saw his team not as resources to be used and discarded but as humans to be valued and supported. He understood that behind every line of code, every sales pitch, every presentation, there was a person with dreams, challenges, and emotions. He didn't view his role as a boss, but as a guide and a mentor—someone who could help his team tap into their full potential.

Raghav took the time to listen to his employees, not just in meetings, but in the corridors, in one-on-one sessions, and during casual conversations. He created an environment where vulnerability was not only allowed but encouraged. In team meetings, he would openly share his own challenges, his fears, and his mistakes. By doing so, he set the tone for the rest of the company. He encouraged his team to embrace failure as a natural part of growth—not something to be ashamed of, but something to be learned from.

The results were immediate and profound. Productivity skyrocketed, not because Raghav demanded it, but because his employees felt truly seen and valued. They didn't work harder simply because they were incentivized by bonuses or the fear of being reprimanded—they worked harder because they felt connected to the company's mission. They felt that their contributions mattered. They knew that their well-being was taken into consideration, and that they weren't just another number on a spreadsheet.

But the impact of Raghav's leadership extended far beyond just performance metrics. Trust and loyalty flourished within the company. People stayed at SilverSutra not just because they were paid well, but because they felt a deep sense of belonging. They felt invested in the company's vision and in each other's success. Employees didn't just work for Raghav—they worked with him. They understood that SilverSutra was more than just a company—it was a community, a family.

As SilverSutra continued to grow, Raghav found himself speaking publicly about his approach to leadership. He didn't stand in front of audiences touting his company's profitability or innovation. Instead, he told stories—not about the numbers, but about the people behind the success. He spoke about the team members who had grown within the company, who had taken on challenges, and who had learned from their failures. He shared stories of how empathy had shaped the culture at SilverSutra and how it had led to greater creativity, collaboration, and resilience.

The message resonated. It wasn't just tech entrepreneurs who were listening—it was leaders from all industries, from healthcare to education, from finance to the arts. They saw something in Raghav's approach that they could replicate in their own organizations. They realized that the traditional models of leadership were outdated, and that empathy and compassion were not signs of weakness but of strength. More and more companies reached out to Raghav, curious to learn how they could integrate empathy into their own cultures. They wanted to know how SilverSutra had built a business that was both profitable and people-centered, and how they could do the same.

At first, Raghav had simply wanted to build a company that was different—one that reflected his values and his desire to create something meaningful. But over time, he began to realize that his impact extended far beyond the walls of SilverSutra. He was building a new kind of empire—one that wasn't built on control or fear, but on compassion and trust.

In a world where success was often defined by how many people a leader could command, Raghav was redefining what it meant to be successful. To him, legacy wasn't built on dominance. It wasn't about being at the top, with others beneath you. It was about building something that could last, something that could grow, and something that could change lives—not just through products or services, but through the way people were treated along the way.

And as Raghav looked back on his journey—on the pain that had led him to this point, on the rejection he had faced, and on the lessons he had learned—he understood the true power of empathy. It wasn't just a soft skill. It was the foundation of everything he had built. It was the key to his success, and it was the thing that would ultimately shape his legacy.

Because in the end, Raghav realized that what truly mattered wasn't how much money SilverSutra made or how many products it sold. What mattered was the impact it had on the people it served. And as long as he continued to lead with empathy, that impact would be immeasurable.

He wasn't just building a company. He was building an empire. An empire that would stand as a testament to the power of kindness, connection, and human potential.

1. **Building Empires**

   Written Exercises:

   * **Empire Vision Blueprint**: Describe in detail what your "empire" looks like in 10 years—career, business, impact, and legacy.

   * **5 Pillars of My Empire**: List the five strongest values or habits that will support your dream empire.

   * **Great Leaders' Reflection**: Choose a great empire builder (e.g., Elon Musk, Shivaji Maharaj, Oprah Winfrey) and write what you'd learn from their mindset.

   Practical Exercises:

   * **Mini Empire Map**: Draw a visual map showing different elements of your empire—team, product, customers, influence.

   * **Empire Journal**: Maintain a daily log of one action you took toward your big vision.

   * **Future Self Letter**: Write a letter from your future self (10 years ahead), describing how you built your empire.

   * **One Empire Move Daily**: Set a 5-minute ritual to make 1 empire-building move every day (learning, networking, creating, etc.).

2. **Empathy**

   Written Exercises:

   * **Walk in Their Shoes**: Choose someone whose views/life you don't understand. Write a paragraph imagining their daily experience.

   * **Empathy Story**: Recall a time someone showed you empathy. How did it impact you?

✳ **Silent Suffering List**: List people around you who might be suffering silently — and what small act you can do to help.

Practical Exercises:

✳ **Active Listening Drill**: Pair up. One speaks about a personal topic, the other listens silently, then reflects back what they heard — no advice or interruptions.

✳ **Emotion Cards**: Pick random emotional scenarios and respond with a statement showing understanding and kindness.

✳ **Service Task**: Perform a small random act of kindness today and reflect on how it made both of you feel.

✳ **Empathy Circle**: Share a personal challenge in a group circle; others respond with "I understand" statements, not solutions.

3. **Walking Through Fire**

Written Exercises:

✳ **My Firewalk Story**: Write about a time you went through intense challenges and what helped you survive.

✳ **Strength Under Pressure**: Describe how hardship shaped you into a stronger version of yourself.

✳ **Fire-to-Force Reflection**: Write 3 lines each on: The Fire I Walked, The Scar It Left, The Strength I Gained.

Practical Exercises:

✳ **Hot Seat Storytelling**: In a group, each person tells one "walked through fire" experience that shaped their life.

* **Cold Water Practice**: Dip hands or feet in cold water while focusing on breath — train the mind to handle discomfort calmly.

* **Firewalk Visualization**: Close your eyes and imagine walking barefoot over hot coals. With each step, mentally burn away fear and self-doubt.

* **Symbolic Burn Ritual**: Write your greatest fear on paper. Burn it in a safe container as a symbol of release.

ECHOES OF CELEBRATION

The grand ballroom, once filled with the frenzy of music, speeches, and clinking glasses, had settled into a more subdued harmony. The lights, now dimmed slightly, cast a soft glow across the room. Raghav walked through the crowd, the hum of conversation around him taking on a different quality. The applause that had greeted him earlier, as he made his speech, had faded into the background. What remained was something quieter, more meaningful—connection. It was a collection of small moments: shared smiles, whispered conversations, and the simple warmth of people coming together.

The celebration, as extravagant and meticulously planned as it had been, no longer felt like the central focus. What had started as a reflection of his success now seemed secondary. Raghav's eyes drifted from face to face as he walked through the hall, and he felt a deep sense of peace. The glittering decorations and the lavish cake no longer mattered in the way they once might have. It wasn't about the accolades or the applause. It was about the people. It was about the relationships and the connections that had grown through the years.

As he moved through the crowd, he overheard snippets of conversation. An old colleague, someone from the early days of SilverSutra, laughed with a group about the time they had almost missed a crucial deadline and how they'd pulled together to make it work at the last minute. That was the beauty of the journey—

they had all been there together, through the highs and the lows. They had survived the moments of doubt, the times when the future seemed uncertain, and yet here they were, celebrating not just the company's success but their shared experience.

Raghav's thoughts shifted to a quiet corner of the room where he saw a former employee, someone who had left the company years ago. She approached him, her eyes filled with gratitude. "I just wanted to thank you, Raghav," she said softly. "For believing in me when I didn't believe in myself. You gave me the chance to grow, and I'll never forget that."

The sincerity in her words hit Raghav like a wave, and he realized in that moment that the true value of his work, his leadership, and his company wasn't measured by the profit margins or the stock prices—it was measured by the lives he had touched. It was the quiet moments, the unspoken connections, that truly defined his journey.

Raghav had always been someone who chased success—who believed that the louder the celebration, the greater the achievement. But standing there, surrounded by familiar faces, he saw something different. He didn't need the world's applause to know he had made a difference. The validation he had so desperately sought in the past was already present in the people whose lives had been shaped by his choices.

It was a profound realization. Success, he now understood, was not a singular moment of glory. It was not the flash of cameras or the gathering of an audience to sing his praises. Success was found in the ripple effects of his actions, in the people who had been empowered by his belief in them. The night, the celebration, wasn't about him anymore. It was about everyone who had contributed to the tapestry of his journey, everyone who had been part of SilverSutra's story. It was about the team, the employees, the partners, the mentors, and even the clients whose trust had helped build the foundation of the company.

Raghav paused for a moment, allowing himself to savor the stillness of the room. The music was soft, the conversations intimate, and the energy in the air had changed from a celebration of success to one of shared gratitude. The people around him weren't just colleagues or friends; they were family. They had supported each other through challenges, celebrated each other's victories, and held each other up in moments of failure. Their stories were intertwined with his in ways he hadn't fully realized until now.

His gaze shifted toward his team—those who had been with him from the very beginning. They stood together, a group of people who had once sat around a table with little more than dreams and a belief in the impossible. They had weathered the early storms, had fought through moments of doubt and fear, and had helped SilverSutra evolve into something that had not only achieved success but had also fostered a culture of care, of empathy, and of deep connection.

Raghav approached them, and they greeted him with smiles and laughter, but there was something different in the air. It wasn't just pride in their work or the company's growth; it was a shared sense of purpose and fulfillment. They had built something together—not just a business, but a legacy. They had built a space where everyone could thrive, where every individual felt seen and valued. And now, as Raghav stood among them, he felt a deep sense of gratitude for the journey they had shared.

In that moment, it was clear to him that true leadership wasn't about seeking validation—it was about creating a space where others could shine. It was about lifting people up, empowering them to grow, and creating an environment where they felt seen and heard. It was about acknowledging the collective effort that went into every success, every milestone, every step forward. Raghav's greatest achievement was not the empire he had built but the impact he had made on the lives of the people who had worked alongside him.

As the night wore on and the celebration came to a gentle close, Raghav found himself reflecting on the journey that had brought him to this point. The highs had been incredible, the challenges unforgettable. But it was the connections, the relationships, and the stories that mattered most. They were the true legacy of his work.

Raghav had learned that true celebration wasn't about grandeur or applause. It was about gratitude — gratitude for the people who had walked with him every step of the way. It was about recognizing that his journey was never just about him. It was about the impact he had made on others, the lives he had touched, and the difference he had helped create in the world.

As the last guests filtered out of the ballroom, Raghav stood there for a moment, watching the empty room. The echoes of celebration lingered in the air, not as noise, but as a quiet reminder of the connections that had been forged, the bonds that had been strengthened, and the love that had been shared. In that silence, he found everything he had been seeking: not applause, not validation, but the profound knowledge that his work had mattered — that it had made a difference.

The night wasn't about him anymore. It was about all the lives intertwined with his journey. And that, he realized, was the truest celebration of all.

1. **Echoes of Celebration**

   Written Exercises:

   * **Milestone Memoir**: Write about a recent achievement — what it meant to you, and how it deserves to echo.

   * **Celebration Reflection Journal**: Reflect on how past celebrations influenced team morale or your personal motivation.

   * **Victory Poem/Paragraph**: Pen a short poem or paragraph titled *"When Victory Echoed"* to describe the emotional aftermath of success.

   Practical Exercises:

   * **Echo Wall**: Create a wall (physical or digital) where team members write one thing they are proud of from a recent success.

   * **Sound of Success**: Record a voice note or short video message expressing joy over success and send it to the team.

   * **Memory Capsule**: Collect small mementos (photos, quotes, doodles) from the celebration and store them in a shared memory folder or envelope.

2. **Success Sharing with Stakeholders**

   Written Exercises:

   * **Gratitude Letters**: Write a thank-you note to stakeholders (team, clients, partners) acknowledging their role in your success.

   * **Stakeholder Impact Chart**: List key stakeholders and describe how their involvement contributed to specific results.

* **Success Story Brochure**: Draft a 1-page newsletter-style write-up highlighting recent wins and the people behind them.

Practical Exercises:

* **Appreciation Meet**: Host a 15-minute gratitude session (in-person or virtual) just to acknowledge stakeholder efforts.

* **Stakeholder Spotlight**: Feature one stakeholder per week on social media or internal platforms with a success shoutout.

* **Feedback Celebration Loop**: Share success updates and ask stakeholders: "How can we do better together next time?"

3. **Celebrating for Gaining More**

Written Exercises:

* **Reflection Prompt**: "How does celebrating each step increase my motivation and vision for bigger achievements?" Write 150 words.

* **Success = Energy Journal**: Track how you feel before and after celebrating—even small wins—for 3 days.

* **Gain List from Past Celebrations**: Write 3 ways in which past celebrations brought new opportunities, connections, or confidence.

Practical Exercises:

* **Post-Success Vision Board**: After celebrating, create a vision board with what you want to achieve next.

* **Power-Up Ritual**: After every major win, practice a celebration ritual (a team cheer, coffee treat, or a shared dance moment) to build momentum.

✳ **Celebration-for-Goals Meet**: Share one success with your team and immediately set a bigger collective goal, linking celebration to purpose.

FINDING BRILLIANCE IN SOLITUDE

The next morning, long after the lights had dimmed and the guests had departed, Raghav sat alone in his study. The bustling celebration of the previous night felt like a distant echo now. The laughter, the music, the clinking of glasses—all of it had faded into the background. What remained was a profound stillness, not an emptiness, but a space filled with clarity.

He sat at his desk, the faint morning light filtering through the curtains, casting soft shadows on the walls. The room was quiet, the only sound the steady rhythm of his breath and the occasional rustle of paper as he moved. This was his moment of solitude—the kind of solitude he had learned to cherish, not fear.

In the silence, Raghav found himself not reflecting on the triumphs of the previous night, nor on the future that awaited him. Instead, his thoughts turned inward. He reflected on the journey he had traveled to get here. He remembered the early mornings of doubt, the sleepless nights when the weight of his ambitions felt too heavy to bear. He thought of the quiet moments when he had taught himself the skills he needed to succeed, reading late into the night, absorbing knowledge that would later shape the vision for SilverSutra.

But more than anything, he remembered the breakthroughs—those small, quiet moments of realization that had come when no one was watching, when there were no applause or accolades. It was in these solitary moments that his mind had found clarity, where the chaos of the world had faded away, and he could hear his own thoughts more clearly. These moments of solitude, he realized, had not been signs of isolation. They had been opportunities for self-discovery.

In the past, Raghav had feared being alone. He had seen solitude as a void, something to be avoided. He feared that in those quiet moments, he might lose his way, that the absence of noise and external validation would make him question his own worth. For so long, he had craved the recognition of others, the applause, the celebrations, the validation that he was on the right path. But now, he saw things differently.

Solitude had never meant being lost. It had always been a space to reconnect with himself. It was in solitude that he had learned to listen—not just to the world, but to his own heart. It was in these moments that his ideas had been born. They hadn't come from the noisy debates or the crowded conference rooms, but from the quiet recesses of his mind, where he could think deeply, without distraction.

As he sat in his study, Raghav began to understand something profound: brilliance didn't always have to be loud or visible. It didn't always come in the form of big speeches or flashy accomplishments. Brilliance often showed itself quietly, steadily, like a small ember glowing in the dark. It was the quiet perseverance that had carried him through the toughest moments of his journey, the small decisions made in silence that had built the foundation for his success.

He thought back to the early days of SilverSutra, when no one knew his name, when the company was just an idea on paper. He had spent countless hours alone in front of his computer, coding, strategizing, learning new concepts, and refining his vision. No one had seen the work he put in behind the scenes. There had been no applause, no accolades—just the steady, quiet effort of building something from the ground up. And yet, it was in those moments that the seeds of his success had been planted.

Now, as he sat in the stillness, he realized that the very solitude he had once feared was the same space that had nurtured his creativity, his resilience, and his growth. It was where he had discovered his true self—beyond the titles, beyond the recognition, beyond the expectations of others. It was in solitude that he had truly found his voice.

Raghav smiled softly to himself. He had spent so many years chasing after external validation, thinking that it was the key to success. But now, he understood that the true key to brilliance lay within. It wasn't about seeking approval from others—it was about trusting in his own abilities, listening to his own instincts, and embracing the quiet moments that allowed his ideas to grow and evolve.

He had learned that brilliance didn't need to shine bright to be real. It could glow quietly, steadily, from within. It was like the steady beat of a heart, the constant hum of life that went unnoticed by most, but was essential to everything that existed. His success, he realized, had never been about the noise. It had always been about the quiet, unspoken moments—the ones that had allowed him to connect with his true self and with the deeper purpose that guided him.

In this moment of reflection, Raghav felt a deep sense of peace. He no longer needed to prove himself. He had already achieved what he had set out to do—not just in terms of building a successful company, but in terms of understanding himself, his values, and his vision. He had discovered that the greatest breakthroughs often came when he was alone, when he could strip away the distractions and reconnect with what truly mattered.

He looked out the window, the sun rising higher in the sky, its light gently flooding the room. The day was beginning, but Raghav felt no rush. He understood now that true brilliance wasn't something that could be rushed or forced. It was something that grew slowly, steadily, over time, nurtured by moments of solitude and reflection.

As he sat back in his chair, he felt a deep sense of gratitude for the solitude that had allowed him to discover his own brilliance. He no longer feared being alone. In fact, he welcomed it. It was in those quiet moments that he had found his truest self, and it was in solitude that he had learned to trust the whispers of his heart.

Raghav closed his eyes for a moment, allowing himself to simply *be*. In that stillness, he knew that he had everything he needed to continue forward. Not just as a businessman or a leader, but as a person who had found peace, purpose, and brilliance in the quiet corners of his own soul.

And in that stillness, he was finally at home.

1. Brilliance

Written Exercises:

* **My Brilliance Journal**: Write 5 things you do exceptionally well — and one moment you truly shined.

* **Brightest Hour Story**: Describe a time when your skills, passion, and action aligned perfectly — what was the result?

* **Brilliance Manifesto**: Compose a personal statement starting with "My brilliance lies in…" and explain how it will impact the world.

Practical Exercises:

* **Spotlight Speech**: Record a 1-minute video or voice note where you speak confidently about your core brilliance.

* **Brilliance Collage**: Collect images/words from magazines or the internet that represent your strengths and create a visual board.

* **Brilliance in Action**: Choose one skill you're proud of, and perform it today for others to benefit or witness.

2. Solitude Power

Written Exercises:

* **Power in Silence**: Reflect and write on this prompt: "What does silence teach me about myself?"

* **Solitude Inventory**: List the best ideas, decisions, or realizations you've had while alone.

* **Solitude vs. Loneliness Chart**: Create a two-column chart to understand the empowering and draining aspects of being alone.

Practical Exercises:

* **Silent Hour Practice**: Spend 1 hour without phone, media, or talking—just observing thoughts. Journal insights afterward.

* **Solo Date**: Take yourself on a walk, coffee outing, or to a park alone. Focus on presence, not distraction.

* **Nature Connection**: Sit alone in nature for 15 minutes. Just breathe, observe, and reconnect.

3. **Alone is Powerful**

Written Exercises:

* **When I Rose Alone**: Write a short story about a time you stood strong alone and made a difference.

* **Alone Doesn't Mean Weak**: Write 3 affirmations that celebrate your independence and personal strength.

* **"Lone Lion" Letter**: Write a fictional letter from a lone lion to a cub explaining the strength found in solitude.

Practical Exercises:

* **Independence Day**: Plan a whole day (or half-day) where you intentionally do things alone—work, eat, reflect.

* **Solo Problem Solver**: Choose a challenge you're facing and brainstorm 3 possible solutions independently before asking others.

* **Mirror Motivation**: Stand before a mirror and say aloud: "I am powerful even when I'm alone. My vision leads me."

AWAKENING THE INNER WARRIOR

As Raghav sat back in the stillness of his study, the weight of the years seemed to settle into his bones. It was in these quiet moments of reflection that he realized how much he had been shaped by his inner battles. Rejection, self-doubt, burnout—all the trials he had faced, both externally and internally, had not been barriers to his success. They had been forges, slowly and silently shaping a spirit stronger than he had ever imagined.

This was no warrior driven by ego or conquest. The warrior spirit that had grown within him was far more subtle, and yet infinitely more powerful. It wasn't built on fighting battles with others or standing over victories. No, this warrior was forged through persistence, emotional truth, and a deep sense of purpose. It wasn't about being invincible or immune to the storms; it was about the act of surviving, of rising after every fall.

Raghav had faced storms—not with the usual armor of pride or arrogance, but with a quiet openness. Every rejection, every sleepless night, every moment of failure had become his battleground, and each time he got back up, he proved to himself that he was stronger than the world had allowed him to believe.

What had once seemed like his greatest vulnerabilities—his willingness to feel pain, his willingness to open his heart to others—had turned out to be his greatest strengths. He had learned to face his emotions rather than hide from them. He had embraced his fears, not as obstacles, but as teachers. And slowly, piece by piece, he had forged a new kind of strength: the strength to be vulnerable, to be truthful with himself, and to never give up, no matter how many times the world tried to push him down.

This strength, Raghav realized, had never been about brute force or the need to outpace others. It was about balance. It was about finding peace in the chaos, clarity in the confusion, and purpose in the pain. His journey had never been a sprint. It had been a slow, steady evolution — each lesson building upon the last, each struggle strengthening his resolve.

With this realization came a shift in his approach. No longer was he focused solely on business or building something for the world to admire. He wasn't chasing legacy anymore. He was living it, daily, through others.

As Raghav had grown, he had begun to mentor young founders — those just starting on their journeys. But his guidance wasn't rooted in business plans, spreadsheets, or revenue forecasts. His lessons came from life. He spoke of resilience, of facing one's own fears, and of embracing the pain that inevitably came with growth.

He would tell them:

* "Let pain be your teacher."

* "Let fear guide your questions."

* "Let compassion define your edge."

These weren't just business strategies. They were life strategies. Raghav had learned that it was not the external world that shaped success. It was the inner world — the mental and emotional landscape — that determined a person's ability to create, to lead, and to persevere. He taught them that the most important battles were the ones fought within, and that true success was not measured by wealth or recognition, but by the strength of one's character and the depth of one's compassion.

Through this, Raghav had come to understand that his strength was rooted not in what he had built, but in how he had evolved, how he had managed to stay grounded while everything around him had shifted. In every moment of doubt, he had chosen to grow, to stay open, and to be vulnerable. And in doing so, he had become the kind of leader he had always dreamed of being: one who was not afraid to show his flaws, to admit when he didn't have the answers, and to lead with empathy rather than power.

LEGACY OF THE UNDERVALUED

As Raghav looked back on his journey, the things he once considered markers of success — awards, accolades, even the wealth that had come with SilverSutra's growth — no longer seemed as important. Yes, they were achievements, but they were not his greatest legacy. His true achievement lay in something far more profound.

Raghav realized that his most important work was not in building a successful company, but in creating a space where people who had been overlooked, dismissed, or underestimated could thrive. His greatest legacy was the home he had built for misfits, dreamers, and doubters — the people who had once felt like they didn't belong anywhere. He had helped them find their value, to see themselves for who they truly were, and in doing so, he had learned to see his own value.

SilverSutra had never just been a company. It had been a sanctuary for the overlooked, a place where people were given a chance to shine, to express their ideas, and to be heard. Raghav had cultivated a culture where empathy was the currency, where vulnerability was encouraged, and where growth wasn't just about professional achievements but about personal evolution. It was a place where people didn't have to be perfect; they just had to be real. And in their realness, they found strength.

As he looked at the faces of those who had worked with him through the years, Raghav saw more than just employees or colleagues. He saw a mosaic of stories, of people who had fought their own battles, who had faced their own doubts, and who had found a home in a company that cared more about who they were than what they could achieve.

Legacy, Raghav realized, wasn't a monument made of stone or metal. It was a mosaic—a living, breathing collection of small, quiet acts of courage and kindness. It was in the way he had chosen to treat others, in the way he had led not by authority, but by empathy. It was in the way he had created a space where people could grow, not just professionally, but personally.

And that legacy was far more powerful than any accolade, any award, or any amount of money. It was the impact he had made on others—the way he had helped them believe in themselves, the way he had created a ripple effect of kindness, empathy, and compassion that extended far beyond the walls of SilverSutra.

In this realization, Raghav felt a deep sense of peace. He no longer needed the world to understand his journey or to recognize his achievements. He had lived it fully, on his own terms, with compassion at the center of everything he did. And that, he understood, was enough.

The journey wasn't about proving himself anymore. It was about continuing to live with purpose, continuing to help others find their own strength, and continuing to build a legacy that would live on long after he was gone—not in the buildings, not in the products, but in the lives he had touched.

And so, Raghav's story wasn't just one of triumph over external obstacles. It was a story of triumph over the internal battles — the ones we all face, the ones we all try to ignore. It was a story of the warrior within, the warrior who doesn't conquer, but who endures. The warrior who rises again and again, not through force, but through compassion, persistence, and truth.

That was Raghav's true legacy. And it was a legacy that would continue to grow, not in the recognition of others, but in the quiet, powerful impact he had on the world.

1. **Awakening the Inner Warrior**

    Written Exercises:

    ✳ **Inner Warrior Letter**: Write a letter from your 'Inner Warrior' to your current self, guiding you through present challenges.

    ✳ **Warrior Trigger List**: List 5 experiences where you showed courage, resilience, or stood up for what was right.

    ✳ **Battle Readiness Journal**: Describe your biggest inner enemy (e.g., fear, self-doubt) and how you plan to defeat it.

    Practical Exercises:

    ✳ **Warrior Pose Practice**: Hold a power stance (like a superhero pose) for 2 minutes while repeating your chosen affirmation.

    ✳ **Obstacle = Opportunity Drill**: Take one current struggle and reframe it as a battle you are preparing to win. Write the strategy.

    ✳ **Symbolic Warrior Object**: Choose or create a physical object (stone, coin, badge) that symbolizes your inner warrior and keep it with you.

2. **From Quiet Past to Victorious Future**

    Written Exercises:

    ✳ **Past vs Future Journal**: In two columns, write "Who I Was" vs "Who I Am Becoming." Include emotions, beliefs, and actions.

    ✳ **Victory Vision Essay**: Describe your victorious future in vivid detail—what you see, feel, do, and how others respond.

✳ **The Transition Timeline**: Map 3 key turning points that shifted your life from passive to powerful.

Practical Exercises:

✳ **Silent Strength Moment**: Spend 10 minutes reflecting silently on past pain, then say aloud: "This made me rise."

✳ **Transformation Video**: Record a short video where you acknowledge your quiet past, declare who you are now, and set your future vision.

✳ **Past Self Letter**: Write a compassionate letter to your past self—thank them, forgive them, and motivate them.

3. **Rising Above All**

Written Exercises:

✳ **Phoenix Affirmation Writing**: Complete and repeat 3 affirmations: "I rise above...," "I am not defined by...," "I become greater when..."

✳ **The Rising Story**: Write about one moment you felt completely down—and how you stood up anyway.

✳ **Above All Mantra**: Create your own power mantra for rising above negativity, limitations, or external pressure.

Practical Exercises:

✳ **Resistance Workout**: Engage in a physical or mental task that challenges you. Finish it while telling yourself "I rise above this."

✳ **Rise Up Challenge**: Identify something you've been avoiding. Take one bold step toward it today.

✱ **Skyline Visualization**: Close your eyes and imagine yourself rising above a city skyline—symbolizing your growth. Breathe in strength, breathe out fear.

YOU DID IT!

Wow! You made it to the end, and what an epic journey it has been! I can't thank you enough for coming along with me on this excursion into the unexplored! This book was crafted with love, sweat, and a sprinkle of insanity, all with you in mind. Whether you've marked pages, scribbled notes, or just allowed the words to wash over you,

I hope you found pieces of yourself in this narrative. As you close the cover, let the ideas leap off the page and dance in your mind. The world outside is brimming with opportunities to put these revelations into action. Think of it as a treasure map leading you to new horizons, ready to be explored. I hope I've stirred some questions, ignited a passion, or even opened doors you didn't know existed.

This is just the beginning, and I encourage you to take everything you've learned here and spread the words like wildfire. Share your thoughts, your critiques, and the newfound knowledge with others. Immerse yourself in discussions that challenge norms and stir up debates — be the catalyst for change! Remember that the quest for understanding doesn't stop here; it's a lifelong adventure. Hold onto the fire of curiosity and never stop exploring.

Society is a complex web of ideas, and your unique perspective matters. So, go out into the world with your armor of wisdom, bravado, and a hint of mischief. Embrace the questions life throws at you and seek answers with grit and determination. Together, we can weave a fabric of curiosity, learning, and growth that transcends the pages of this book. I'm thrilled to have shared this journey with you.

Your presence and engagement have made every moment of this writing process worthwhile. As you step back into your life, carry forward the inspirations and revelations from these chapters. Keep exploring, engaging, and questioning the world around you. We are all in this together, and I can't wait to see how you translate the magic from these pages into your everyday life! Now go, create ripples of curiosity wherever you wander!

With all my enthusiasm,

– ARJ Daund